Tomato Growing
A Beginners Guide to Plump & Juicy Tomatoes
(B&W Version)

By

Kendra K

Table of Contents

Introduction

Tomatoes have been around in one form or another for a very long time; they go way back. It is believed that this fruit was already domesticated by the Aztecs around 500 AD. It is therefore native to the Americas. However, it took another 2000 years for tomatoes to be introduced to Europe when the early explorers encountered it and brought it back after their expeditions. In the 1540's it was cultivated in Spain and the long process of breeding tomatoes of all shapes, sizes and colors commenced. It was only introduced in Asia during the early 1900's but spread quickly to all parts of the world.

The first tomatoes were yellow and cherry-like, and were aptly called golden apples. Today there are over 500 different varieties grown in the USA alone. They vary in size from small one-bite fruit to large plump tomato varieties. Likewise, they come in many colors, ranging from white, yellow and orange to a bright red, purple and black. Americans on average consume 22 to 24 pounds of this delicious fruit per person every day, making it the most popular agriculture-produce item in the country.

Mother Nature has provided us with this nutritious, healthy fruit and we have taken to it vigorously. Working alongside nature to grow your own is an added boon; not only will you have the freshest tomatoes on your table, you will also benefit from the healing nature of working with the earth and its plants. Not only will working in the garden increase your physical fitness; it has been proven repeatedly that it will help to improve your mental health. Even if you do not have an outside garden, you can still grow your own tomatoes in pots, window boxes or hanging containers.

The American educator and poet John Erskine said, "I have never had so many good ideas day after day as when I worked in the garden." This is the time for the first of hundreds of good ideas to follow. You have always wanted to get closer to nature, now is your opportunity: Start growing your own tomato plants.

In the following chapters, I will tell you exactly how to go about it, how to select the right variety, how to plant them, how to keep your plants healthy and how to preserve your excess tomatoes. It is simple and easier than you imagined. Just follow these basic instructions and you will be enjoying your own homegrown juicy, plump and flavorful tomatoes before the end of the season.

~ Kendra ~

Chapter One

How to Grow Tomatoes

Using Seeds to Grow Tomato Plants

Did you know that there are literally hundreds of different varieties of tomatoes? We are not always aware of this fact because when we visit our local nursery, we may see only twelve or so different tomato plants. However, the variety of tomato seeds that are available is much greater. So, if you want to grow some unusual ones, why not grow them from seeds rather than plants. It is really a simple and easy project as long as you do a little planning.

1.   When to Plant Your Tomato Seeds

First, decide when you want to plant your tomato seedlings into your vegetable garden. If you live in an area where frost occurs, this should take place 2 or 3 weeks after the last frost of the season. Your seeds will need between 6 and 8 weeks to be ready for planting in the garden, which means that you must start growing your tomato seeds 4 to 6 weeks prior to the last frost.

2.   How to Go About It

Use small pots for your seeds. You can start the seeds in either damp soil especially sold for seed starting, or damp peat pellets. The last option is potting soil, also moistened. Plant two seeds into each pot to make sure you do not end up with a pot without a seedling. Not all seeds will germinate.

Look at the measure and size of your seed. Now multiply that by three. You should plant your seeds at this depth. It usually comes to an eighth to a quarter inch deep, depending on which variety you have decided on.

Seeds need warmth to germinate, so place your pots in a warmish area, around seventy to eighty degrees Fahrenheit or twenty one to twenty seven degrees Celsius for faster germination. What works really well, is on top of a kitchen appliance like a refrigerator, which generates heat. The heat that they get from the bottom will help the germination process. Another option is to use heating pads; switched to low, and covered in a towel.

Now all you have to do is sit back and relax. Your seeds will start germinating in seven to fourteen days, depending on the temperature of the area. If you leave your seed containers in a cool area, they will take longer to germinate while a warmer area will make your seeds germinate much faster.

As soon as germination has occurred, your seedlings do not need a heat source any more. However, you should still keep them in a warm place. What they need now are two things. First, they need enough light. If you do not have a window facing south which can provide adequate bright light, use a grow bulb or florescent light. Install this light source some inches above the seedlings. Secondly, the soil must be kept damp and moist at all times. It is best to water the seedlings from the bottom, but if you find this impractical, make sure no water dribbles onto the newly sprouted seedlings when you water them.

When your seedlings have grown somewhat and show one or two true leaves, they need fertilizer. Use only a quarter of the usual strength and dissolve in water.

If your seedlings do not get enough light, they will become leggy. They are stretching themselves towards the light. Rectify this problem by placing them closer to the light source. Otherwise, you should make sure the amounts of light they get, is increased. If you notice that your little plants turn a purple color, it means that they need more fertilizer. Reapply the dissolvable, diluted fertilizer like before. If the stems of your seedlings become mushy and fall over, it means they are suffering from damping off. A soil fungus usually causes this. It can be prevented by good air circulation and using organic soil in your containers.

So, turn your vegetable patch into an unexpected, exceptional garden by choosing a variety of unusual tomatoes to grow from seeds. It is easy and a lot of fun.

Using Cuttings to Grow Tomato Plants

We have all been given a cutting off a perennial, shrub or houseplant we admired at a friend's house and successfully grown it in our own gardens or homes. However, not many people are aware of the fact that quite a few vegetables could be started in the same way. Tomatoes are a perfect example; they can be rooted directly into soil or in water. Want to find out how easy it is? Read on.

You have been eyeing your neighbor's beautiful, lush tomatoes for a while. So why not approach him or her and ask for a cutting from the plant you admire so much. Your neighbor will be flattered and you will end up with your own prize-winning tomatoes.

One of the advantages of using cuttings is that it is cost-effective, since you only have to obtain one plant of a kind and use that to root as many as you like. Another huge advantage is that you save time. Growing tomato plants from seeds may take up to 8 weeks or even more before they can be transplanted into your garden. If you make use of cuttings, you can reduce this time until transplanting to two weeks or less, more so if you keep the cuttings warm.

It is surprisingly easy to grow plants from cuttings and tomatoes especially do not waste any time to grow roots from cuttings. Choose the plant you want to use and select a sucker shoot that does not have any buds on it. Using a sharp set of pruners, cut off the top eight inches of this new growth. You can now place the cutting into a jar of water or otherwise plant it straight away into the soil. In water, roots should appear within seven days and your cutting is ready for the garden.

Cuttings which are planted directly in soil will develop stronger roots. It also means that you save one-step and do not have the extra job of transplanting the cutting later so it makes sense to start the process of propagation in the soil.

How to go about it: Cut off any buds or flowers. Next, get rid of all the leaves at the bottom of your cutting, keeping only two towards the top half. Place your cuttings in a jar with water while you are preparing the soil. They can be planted in pots with peat or any container filled with vermiculite or dampened potting soil. You may even plant them straight into your garden. With a pencil or dowel, make a deep enough hole in the soil. Now insert your cutting into the hole. It should be buried up to the place where you snipped off all the lower leaves.

Place your containers indoors, or outside, as long as it is in an area that is warm. The area should be shaded to protect them from the hot sun. Keep your cuttings moist all the time. They should stay here for about seven days to acclimatize. After a week, gradually move them more and more into the light until the plants are exposed to sunlight for the biggest part of the day. Now they are ready for their bigger, permanent pots or spots in your vegetable garden.

Tomatoes produce their best fruits in their first year. Although they are perennials and will live for many years in a warm climate, their fruit will not be of the same quality. Therefore, it is a good idea to select new cuttings that you can nurture during the winter. Follow the exact steps as set out above. After transplanting your tomato cuttings into their bigger pots, allow them to overwinter in a sunny, warm area until springtime.

Always be careful when you select your cuttings. Choose them from those plants that produce the most and the tastiest tomatoes. Remember that cuttings are virtual clones of their parent plants and will yield the same results.

Tomatoes Grown in Containers and Pots

Not all of us have a large plot to use as a vegetable garden. This should not deter you from growing your favorite tomatoes, though. They have been cultivated in pots and all kinds of containers for many years. Be creative and use the limited space available: Plant your chosen vegetable in planters, window boxes, hanging baskets on your balcony or any kind of container of your choice. Make sure the container is a match for the variety of your choice, take care of your plant and success is guaranteed.

1.   How to Go About It

To grow tomatoes in pots is easy. Keep in mind that the size of the chosen container should match the size of your fully-grown plant. In this way, your plant will yield the best fruit. For example, a window box or hanging basket is best suited for cherry tomatoes or similar smaller varieties. For a larger plant, choose a five-gallon bucket or sturdier planter.

The size of the container is important for various reasons. It should be large enough with ample space for the roots of your plant. Usually a twelve-inch wide pot with a depth also of 12 inches will be suitable for almost all plants. You may also consider bushel baskets or half barrels but any container you decide on should have sufficient drainage.

2.   Different Types of Tomatoes for Containers

Tomato plants come in two types: indeterminate or vining, and determinate or bushy. Both are suitable for containers but the bushy type seems to be preferred by most people, as they are easier to care for. They do not need staking. Remember your choice will also determine the container you use and where you want to place your container. For example, indeterminate tomato plants are not always suitable for window boxes, as they will eventually cover part of your view.

Here is a list of the most common tomatoes used in containers:
- Pixie
- Patio
- Toy Boy
- Tiny Tim
- Floragold
- Micro Tom
- Stakeless
- Early Girl
- Big Boy

3.   How to Go About It

Step 1 is to select the correct potting soil for your pot. It should drain well, so I suggest that you mix it with organic materials such as manure or shavings. The ideal would be to mix perlite, compost, potting soil and peat moss in equal measures.

You can start with your tomato seeds indoors during the early spring. Otherwise, buy the young plants from your nursery as soon as they are available. If you choose the indeterminate kind of tomatoes that require staking, it might be a good idea to add this stake or cage at this stage.

Your containers should be placed in a spot that gets full sun. Check them every day and water them when needed. Weekly watering will usually suffice, but during dry or hot spells, your tomato plants may need watering more frequently. During midsummer, start adding a fertilizer, soluble in water bi-weekly. Continue with the fertilizer right through your plant's growing season.

It is easy to grow tomatoes plants in pots. It will add variety and a fun look to your home, patio, window box or garden and your container plants should produce the same quality and quantity of fruit as those that are grown outdoors.

Indoor Tomatoes and How to Grow Them

Most tomato plants do best during the warmer season and tend to die as soon as colder temperatures arrive. If you do not have your own greenhouse, the arrival of winter need not mean the end of your delicious homegrown tomatoes. Although they may yield slightly less and smaller fruit, you can still enjoy your own tomatoes during the colder months. Make sure to choose the correct varieties that flourish indoors. Take good care of them and you will have the lovely smell of fresh tomatoes in your kitchen all year round.

1. How Do I Grow Tomatoes Plants Indoors

To be able to produce fruit, tomato plants need light for a minimum of eight hours every day, as well as full sun. The indoor temperature should be around 65 degrees Fahrenheit or 18 degrees Celsius.

If you have grown your tomatoes in pots outside during the summer, move them indoors towards the last weeks of the season to preserve them. This way you can save them over a few seasons. As they become older, they will eventually stop yielding fruit but at least you will be able to extend their fruit bearing years.

Here is a quick tip to guarantee an endless supply of fresh tomatoes right through the season: Grow your indoors tomatoes in batches successively, instead of all at the same time. Plant seeds every fortnight and they will start yielding one after the other.

2. How Do I Grow Tomatoes during Winter

Plant your seeds in the containers filled with a starter mix. Do not plant them deeper than a quarter inch, using pots of about six inches. Make sure the containers are well drained and keep their soil moist at all times. Containers should be placed in warm areas, for example on top of your refrigerator. Every two weeks, start one or even two new pots and you will end up with a number of plants during the winter, extending into the early spring.

Germination will start in 5 to 10 days. Now move your pots into an area that is brightly lit, a south facing window is best. Keep the window closed during drafty periods. The temperature should remain around 65 degrees Fahrenheit or 18 degrees Celsius.

Higher temperatures of between 75 and 85 degrees F or 24 to 29 degrees Celsius, will promote early flowering and the best growth. At this stage, you should start with the fertilizer, repeating it every 14 days.

3.　　The Fruit and Flowers of Indoor Tomatoes

In order for plants to be able to produce fruit, pollination must occur and this can cause a dilemma when growing plants indoors. You will have to assist nature in this respect with pollinating by hand. As soon as the flowers bloom, spread the pollen by tapping all the stems of the plant lightly. If you want to make doubly sure, you can insert cotton swabs into every flower in turn.

You want your plant to produce flowers and fruit evenly all around, so be sure to turn the pot or container frequently. It needs sun and light on all sides. Inspect your plants regularly to stake them when needed lest the fruit becomes too heavy for the branches and break them. You can expect your winter tomatoes to start yielding fruit in around the same length of time as those that grow outdoors.

4.　　Which Tomatoes Varieties to Grow Indoors

Certain tomatoes present themselves better as indoor plants than others. Therefore, to ensure success, you have to select the variety that will perform best under these conditions. The smaller, upright varieties are better suited since they take up less space in your home.

Here are a few to choose from:
- Tiny Tim
- Red Robin
- Florida Petite

- Toy Boy

Something different you may consider choosing are those varieties that hang down. These create a spectacular display with arching branches full of fruit. Try Yellow Pear that bears delicious golden tomatoes or Burpee Basket King with its smaller red tomatoes. The latter is of the trailing plant.

When you make your selection for your indoor garden, consider growth habit, fruit type, size and the ability to bear fruit in these cooler temperatures. Most people prefer Red Robin since it seems to enjoys the indoors and is quite happy to yield wonderful fruit inside the house.

Chapter Two

Some Common Problems

One of the most popular and easiest vegetables that you can grow in your own garden is tomatoes. Growing them is a simple project, but alas, this does not imply that you will not encounter any problems with your tomato plants. Novices expect to experience problems but even expert gardeners sometimes wonder why their tomato plants seem to be dying. What you need is information and knowledge about the common problems that you might expect. Only then will you be able to grow healthy and happy plants.

In this chapter, I will inform you of the problems most commonly encountered by home gardeners. Secondly, I will discuss in more detail the pests and diseases which most often plaque tomato plants. Lastly, I will provide you with the best practical solutions for handling these problems.

Diseases in Tomato Plants

Diseases are the main cause for failure when growing tomato plants. The reason for this is their susceptibility to all kinds of afflictions. The following is a list of the most common diseases as well as a short description of the symptoms:

- Altemaria Canker: The leaves, stems and fruit show brownish depressed spots.
- Bacterial Canker: The leaves wilt, then start turning yellow, later becoming brown and ultimately die, starting at the bottom.
- Bacterial Speck: The fruit and leaves show small brownish dots surrounded by yellow rings.

- Bacterial Spot: The leaves show black, wet spots which later start to decompose and then leave holes in the leaves.
- Cucumber Mosaic Virus: Your entire tomato plant is stunted and the leaves are thinner than they should be.
- Early Blight: The leaves develop big black spots of an irregular shape and yellow rings all around them.
- Fusarium Crown Rot: The more mature leaves turn brown, and then the entire plant turns a brownish color. The stems too exhibit brown lines.
- Fusarium Wilt: Despite the correct administering of water, the plants wilt.
- Gray Leaf-Spot: Leaves develop small brownish spots. The spots start to rot and eventually leave tiny holes in all the foliage.
- Late Blight: The fruits of the plant show indented spots, the leaves turn papery, and a pale brown color.
- Leaf Mold: When you turn the leaves over, you will notice light yellow or green spots. Eventually the whole leave will turn a yellow color.
- Powdery Mildew: All the leaves of the plant are covered in a powdery white layer.
- Septoria Leaf-Spot: Mostly the older leaves will develop grey and brown spots.
- Southern Blight: The plant will wilt. Brown spots will show on the stems of the plant right at soil level or quite near it.
- Spotted Wilt: The leaves form spots in the shape of bull's eyes. The whole plant is stunted.
- Timber Rot: All the stems of the plant will be hollow and be covered in mouldy spots. These spots will also appear on the leaves.
- Tobacco Mosaic: The leaves of the plant are patchy with a bright green and yellow color.
- Verticillium Wilt: Despite the proper watering regimen, the plant wilts.

Environmental Issues

We have looked at the different types of diseases that may kill tomato plants. However, these are not the only causes for failure in tomatoes. Equally important for success are other issues like the amount of water the plant gets, whether too much or too little, a lack of enough light, and poor soil.

Tomato plants need just the correct amount of water. Too much or too little water will have the same results: The plant will appear wilted and the leaves will turn yellow. How do you determine the correct amount of water for your plant? Simply by examining the soil and using your common sense. If the soil cracks, or appears dusty and dry, you are under -watering. If there is standing water visibly in the soil, or if it looks swampy, you are definitely over-watering.

Plants need good soil to be able to grow. If your soil is sub-standard, the quality and quantity of the fruit will be poor and your entire plant will be underdeveloped with poor growth. The reason is that they lack proper nutrients and just like humans who cannot grow well without proper food; plants also need enough nutrients to be in good health.

Finally, yet importantly, tomato plants, like most fruit bearing plants need plenty of sunlight. Tomato plants in particular usually need a minimum of 5 hours of sunlight every day in order to survive. Anything less will result in a stunted plant that may eventually die.

Tomato Pests

Tomato plants may be damaged or even killed by a variety of garden pests. These pests typically target the leaves or fruit of the plants. The following is a list of pests that damage the leaves:
- Blister Beetles
- Aphids

- Colorado Potato Bugs
- Cabbage Loopers
- Leaf miners
- Flea Beetles
- Thrips
- Stink Bugs
- White Flies
- Tomato Hornworms

The following is a list of pests that target the fruit of plants:
- Slugs
- Rodents
- Tomato Pinworm
- Tomato Fruit Worm
- Tomato Budworm
- Vegetable Leaf Miner

You cannot deal with the problems that affect your plant if you do not know what is causing it. Be vigilant and inspect your tomato plants regularly. The sooner you become aware of a problem, the sooner you can remedy it. Even experienced gardeners often encounter problems; it is a common occurrence amongst tomato growers.

Tomatoes That Split or Crack

This is a very common problem for all tomato gardeners. You might be under the impression that your plants are healthy and without any diseases or pests but then discover that the fruit starts to split or crack. This can be quite disheartening, especially if you do not know the reasons why it is happening.

Why are My Tomatoes Splitting?

Tomatoes prefer steady temperatures. Newly transplanted tomatoes, particularly, may suffer from fluctuations in temperature during springtime. One way to prevent your plants from suffering is to add mulch to the soil. Organic mulch for example wood chips is ideal. The moisture will be preserved and mulch may even prevent diseases from spreading.

A long rainy period followed by a very dry spell can cause some of the fruit to crack or split. The human skin will eventually split if it does not receive adequate moisture and this principle applies to tomatoes as well. They need enough water to stay juicy and plump. Without it, their skin will show cracks. If they receive a lot of water after a dry period, the fruit will fill with moisture that will cause the cracks in the skin of the tomato to split open just like a water balloon that has been overfilled with water.

How Do I Prevent My Tomatoes From Cracking?

A cracked skin is a danger to the tomato fruit and not merely a question of aesthetics. Our skin is able to form a crust to protect it from bacteria entering into our bloodstream but the tomato does not have this luxury. Fungus and bacteria may enter through the crack, causing the fruit to rot. Pests can now easily access the fruit and damage it. The best way to prevent your tomatoes from splitting is to give them the correct amount of water. I suggest around one or two inches per week. They should be evenly watered.

If you plan on being absent from your home and cannot find anyone to tend your plants, it is wise to set up a system for watering them regularly. This can be done with a timer. You certainly do not want to arrive home to plants with split fruit after all the loving care you have bestowed on them. A watering system frees you to be absent for long periods while still enjoying healthy lush homegrown tomatoes.

Healthy soil alone does not provide enough nourishment for your plants. You have to fertilize them regularly as well. Read the instructions of your particular fertilizer carefully and apply as instructed. With nourishment in the form of fertilizer, your plants will produce their maximum quantity of fruit and you will end up with enough tomatoes to share with your friends.

Tomatoes with Septoria Leaf Canker

This disease primarily targets members of the tomato plant family and is considered one of the most destructive foliage diseases. The spots on the leaves, especially the older ones, are used to diagnose it. This leaf blotch can easily be recognized and your plant could be affected at any time during its development. During wet spells, the Septoria fungus is deposited on the leaves, after which warmer temperatures helps it to start blooming. Therefore, it flourishes in extended wet humid conditions.

How Do I Identify It

Septoria spots on leaves are small; they are between a sixteenth to a quarter inch in size. The matured spots have light tan colored centers with brown edges. Use your magnifying glass to look for the tiny fruiting bodies right in the middle of every spot. When these bodies ripen, they explode and the fungal spores are spread all over the plant. Although the fruit and stems of the plant will not be affected, the disease will eventually spread to the younger leaves of the plant if not treated in time.

Tomato plants with Septoria Canker experience a lot of stress and will not grow to their full potential. The plant will lose all its foliage as the disease spreads up the stems, which in turn will prevent the plant from absorbing energy from the sun. Without enough energy, the plant will be unhealthy and the quality of the fruit will suffer.

Spetoria on Solanaceous Plants

This disease is not unique to tomato plants. Other members of the family may also be affected, including potato, eggplant, peppers and the tobacco plant. Inedible plants like Jimsonweed, Black Nightshade and Horse Nettle Ground Cherry are often under attack from this disease. The fungus does not live in soil, but needs plant material to survive. It can even be found in the seeds and rhizomes of these plants.

How to Control Septoria Leaf Canker

Septoria lycopersici is the fungus that causes Septoria. During the cold winter months, it hibernates in discarded tomato plant debris and wild plants of the Solanceous family. It is easily spread by rain and wind and needs temperatures between sixty to eighty degrees Fahrenheit, (sixteen to twenty-seven degrees Celsius), to flourish. It is obvious that good, disciplined garden hygiene is essential in combating this disease. What do I mean by that? Clean up and get rid of and all the old plant materials. Change the location where you plant your tomatoes from year to year. It is a quite effective way in which you can prevent diseases from spreading.

When you observe septoria on the leaves of your plant, treat it with fungicides, applying it over a 7 to 10 day period for the best results. Spray the fungicide as soon as the first fruit appears right after the blossoms have dropped. A variety of fungicides sprays are available but the chemicals most often used are maneband chlorothalonil. Copperand ziram products, as well as potassium bicarbonate are also effective in combating this disease. Always follow the directions on the label, as it will tell you how often and which doses to apply.

Little-Leaf Syndrome in Tomatoes

If you notice that the young leaves of your tomato plant are distorted and stunted, your plant if probably suffering from Little-Leaf Disease. In this section, I will explain what this syndrome is and what the causes are.

What Little-Leaf Syndrome Is

Farmers first encountered this disease in southwestern Georgia and northwestern Florida. The name already gives an idea of how this disease manifests. Interveinal chlorosis in the younger leaves occur. They are stunted and fail to produce chlorophyll. Often leaves will be twisted with brittle midribs. The flowers as well as the fruit of the plant will be distorted and failure to fully develop occurs.

The plant will yield fruit that appear flattened and will show cracks lengthwise, from the blossom scar to the calyx. When you cut open the tomatoes, you will notice that they hardly contain any seeds. The disease is easily confused with another one called Cucumber Mosaic Virus, especially if your plants are severely afflicted.

This syndrome is comparable to a disease often found in tobacco plants. The latter is a non-parasitic disease, since the organism that causes the disease does not grow in the tissues of the plant. It is called frenching and often occurs in poorly aerated, wet soil during periods of higher temperatures than usual.

The disease is not unique to tomato and tobacco plants. It has been seen in plants like petunia, eggplant, sorrel, squash, and ragweed.

Causes of Little-Leaf Syndrome

Unfortunately, the etiology or cause of this syndrome is not clear. Scientists who have studied afflicted tomato plants could not detect any viruses. Soil and plant tissue samples that were taken did not reveal any clues as far as the pesticide analysis or nutrients are concerned. At present the agreed theory is that under certain conditions, there seems to be an organism or organisms present which lives on the roots' surfaces of the plant. They exude chemicals that then lead to the distortion of the leaves and the morphing of the flowers and fruit.

Currently three different culprits are considered the likely culprits:
- Aspergillus wentii, a fungus
- Bacillus cereus, also a fungus
- Macrophomina phaseolina, a fungus found in the soil.

This said; the final verdict is not yet out and the exact cause of this disease stays unclear. However, it seems to be more commonplace in alkaline soils with a pH level of more than 6.3, and in neutral soil. It also appears to favor wet areas with high temperatures.

Treatment for Little-Leaf Disease

Until the exact cause of this syndrome is identified, it is very difficult to ascertain how to treat it. Before the culprit is pinpointed, it is uncertain which chemical control should be applied. At present, there are no commercial cultivars that are resistant to this disease, either. Rather plant your tomatoes in those areas in the garden that are not too wet. If you use ammonium sulphate to reduce the pH level of your soil to under 6.3, it may also help to prevent Little-Leaf Disease.

Bumpy Stems or Vines on Tomato Plants

At this point you may feel that the problems you might encounter in your endeavor are too numerous. True, no gardening is completely problem free, but the joy of eventually harvesting and eating your own homegrown tomatoes makes it all worth your while. So, let us continue.

The vines of your tomato plant that have been so nice and smooth until the other day now have bumps all over them. Maybe they resemble acne or white growths. Do not despair; this is a common problem.

What are the White Bumps?

This will surprise you: The growths or bumpy white things you see on the stems and vines of your tomato plants are actually roots. They are a mass of tiny little roots, resembling hairlets that grow all along the stems. If they are covered with soil, they will develop into proper roots but above ground, they turn into nodules. They are descriptively called stem primordial, root initials or adventitious roots and are actually the earliest developing roots.

What Are The Causes of Bumpy Vines?

Roots are part of plants but you may wonder why they grow on the stems and vines of your tomato plant. Well, I have another surprise for you: When people are suffering from stress, they often develop acne. Similarly, the white bumps on your plant are the manifestation of stress. Plants get some of their nutrients from the soil, and these nutrients have to travel all along the vascular system of the plant to reach the leaves, blossoms and fruit. If a blockage occurs somewhere along the line, the plant will experience stress and will then send out auxin, a hormone in the plant itself, to the roots where the blockage occurs. Because of the barrier, the hormones will accumulate and form a bump in the stems of the plant.

A number of stressors can cause bumpy stems in tomato plants. The one most commonly found is excess water. Either you are overwatering your plant or it may be the result of too much rain and a lack of proper drainage. Other stressors include internal injury, root damage, high humidity and irregular cell growth. All these factors may cause stress in the plant and result in the development of root initials. Be aware that these bumps come in different colors and can be either brown, white or green like the vines and stems of the plant.

Exposure to herbicides may be another cause for bumpy stems. Even if you have not made use of herbicide, your neighbor's spraying could have blown over to your side of the fence and affected your plant. Inspect the leaves as soon as you notice swelling anywhere on the vines or stems of the plant. Stunted or curled leaves may be a symptom of exposure to an herbicide. Herbicides often act just like the hormone in the plant, leading to stunted leaves and bumpy vines.

How to Treat Bumpy Stems

Bumps on your tomato plant is not a serious concern and could be ignored almost all the time. They will not harm your plant in any way. Actually, these initial roots may help to strengthen your plant. Cover the lower ones with soil so that they can develop properly and the mature roots will help your plant to grow to its full potential.

However, if the bumps coincide with your plant wilting, it is a sure sign of too much water. Ensure that the soil drains well, especially in areas of high rainfall and never overwater your plant. You are not doing it any favors by giving it an abundance of water.

Another condition, a more severe one, called verticillium or fusarium wilt, may resemble the above-mentioned problem. Browning of the leaves, wilting, stunted growth and black streaks on the stems of the plant are all symptoms of this disease. It can be treated with fungicides, but only if you catch it early enough. If the disease is full blown before it comes to your attention, it is a better idea to get rid of the plant completely. Uproot it and dispose of it, then start a new plant.

Mosaic Virus in Tomato Plants

As we have seen, there are many different diseases which may inflict harm on your tomato plant. Insects may also be on the attack and infest it. Often symptoms are the same as those that are found in other diseases, like defects in nutrition. It becomes even more complicated when the problem you encounter is both related to insects and a virus. The mosaic virus is just such a one.

What is the Mosaic Virus?

This virus can infect your entire plant, from the leaves to the stems. It can also manifest during any stage in its growth. It is called a mosaic virus, as it resembles tiny mosaics on the foliage that gives it a speckled appearance. It looks like an overall mottling on all the leaves. At the full-blown stage, the leaves will look similar to those of a fern; it will have raised areas of dark green and have a blister-like appearance. It could become stunted.

Plant suffering from the mosaic virus will have a reduction of fruit yield. The fruits that do manage to grow will show deformities like dark patches on the inside with dotted yellow blotches as well as necrotic spots on the skin. The virus may infect all sections of the plant, from the stems to the petioles and the leaves.

Other plants may also be affected by the mosaic virus, for example beans, tobacco, squash, cucumber, potatoes, peppers and roses. The virus will rarely kill the plants, but the fruit quantity and quality will be reduced. It is not too easily diagnosed, as it resembles many other afflictions caused by air pollution, herbicides, or mineral deficiencies.

How to Control Mosaic Virus

After hibernating in perennial weeds during the winter and as soon as the temperatures rise, the disease is spread with the help of several insects like leafhoppers, aphids, cucumber beetles and whiteflies. Divisions and cuttings from already infected plants definitely will both be infected. Environmental conditions favorable to the virus will exacerbate the spread and symptoms of the mosaic virus. Not all plants are equally susceptible to the virus.

The disease enters the plant through tiny wounds which can be caused by insect chewing, grafting or mechanical injuries. Plant detritus is known to be the most likely cause of contagion. Any kind of tobacco can transmit the disease through the hands of the person who touches it.

Other than fungal diseases that are easier to treat with chemicals, this virus proves much more problematic. Mosaic virus can survive for as long as fifty years in dried up plant detritus. Under these conditions, you will agree that it is very difficult to eliminate or control the disease. The emphasis is rather on the reduction and elimination of the sources for the virus and the infestation of insects.

The correct hygiene is the best practice to apply for the control of the mosaic virus in tobacco. Keep away from tobacco products like cigarettes while you are working with your tomato plants. Wash your hands constantly or change your gloves. All tools must be sterilized by boiling them for five minutes and afterwards washing them with strong detergents. Bleach is not an effective agent against viral contamination. If you are starting tomato plants from seeds, destroy all seedlings that look stunted or appear distorted and make sure to decontaminate all the tools you used as well as your hands.

You have worked hard to get your tomato plant to grow so nicely and do not have the heart to destroy the entire plant when it becomes infected. Remove all the speckled or yellowed leaves and then destroy them. Make sure to decontaminate all the tools you have used.

The best prevention against tomato mosaic virus is to keep your plants in good health. Give them proper feeding and the correct amount of water and you will have stress-free plants. Discard all possible agents of contamination in the vicinity of the plants, and weed regularly. Get rid of all plant debris around the plants. Be on the lookout for insects that may infest and contaminate them. When you use tools or machinery around your plants, be careful not to harm them in any way as injuries may allow the virus to enter into the plant tissue through cuts or lesions.

If you were unlucky to have cases of the mosaic virus, there are a few things you should do towards the end of the growing season: Remove the entire plant and burn it. Clean the whole area well and do not use that same area again for growing any plants susceptible to the virus, like tomatoes, peppers or cucumbers. In this way, you will not spread the disease in your garden.

Chapter Three

How to Grow Plump Tomatoes

Try to imagine a life without tomatoes. Impossible, is it not. People have been planting and growing these wonderful, delicious fruits for many years and you will be hard-pressed to find a vegetable garden that does not have a few of these wonderful juicy fruits. As I have discussed in the previous chapter, it is not difficult to grow healthy tomato plants, but to enable you to grow the biggest, plumpest fruit, you will need some advice.

A few basic factors play a deciding part in how your tomatoes will turn out. These are the fertility of your soil, the seed quality, the amounts of water you give your plant and lastly how much sunlight they receives. In this chapter, I will provide you with all the secrets of how to grow tomatoes that will make you the envy of all your fellow gardeners.

1.   Choose Varieties with Flavor

Although there are literally hundreds of varieties of tomatoes to choose from, you should be aware that not all varieties would yield juicy, red fruit full of flavor. The first known tomatoes were found around South America. They grew wild and were a lot smaller, much like our cherry tomatoes of today. Neither were they the bright red color we treasure so much today; they were a yellowish, light orange color. Mutations that occurred as time passed, selective breeding as well as modern day hybridization lead to the type of fruit we have today; juicy tomatoes, with a beautiful vibrant red color, large and fleshy.

Even if you discount all the odd shapes and multitude of colors of our inherited tomatoes, there still remain countless modern varieties to choose from. Tomatoes that are commercially cultivated and sold in stores have been developed especially to withstand all the dangers and rigors of the mechanical processes of picking, sorting, including the transportation. The result is tomatoes with thick skins, waxy feel and a flavorless, bland taste.

The tomatoes you grow in your own garden will be handled with care and do not need to withstand such harsh conditions. Therefore, you can select the juiciest, sweetest kind. Maybe you want to grow a few different varieties that you can put to a variety of use, for instance sweet tomatoes for salads, more acidic fruit for salsas, or fleshier ones for grilling.

Amongst the older varieties, choose those with the best flavor, like Burpee's Globe, Aunt Ginny's Purple, Big Ben, McClintock's Big Pink, Brandywine and African Queen. Favorable ones to choose from amongst the hybrids are Crimson Fancy, Glacier, Celebrity, Beefy Boy, Red Sun, Jet Star, Dona, Scarlet Red and Red Sun.

2.   Select Varieties Suited to Your Area

You have made a selection suited to your personal taste and needs. However, that will not be a guarantee for success. An important factor to consider is the climate of the area you live in and the condition of soil in your garden. You cannot change your climatic conditions, which means you have to make your choice to suit the temperatures in your areas. Not all heirloom varieties will yield the same satisfying results in different climatic areas.

People often make the mistake to take the seeds from their favorite tomato plants with them to sow in their new homes just to find out that their tomatoes do not taste like it used to. Not only is it a question of moving to a different zone of your country, but many other conditions will have an influence on the quality of your plants, for example the pH level of the soil, the humidity, wind conditions and rainfall.

Do not be afraid to experiment, with different varieties. Read up on which varieties to scout for, or get information from your local nursery. Speak to the experienced gardeners in the area; they are the ones who will give you the best advice. They have done all the groundwork already; there is no need for you to invent the wheel again.

3.   Start Your Plants Early

Tomatoes will flourish if they have a running start so time your growing schedule wisely. If you live in a colder climate, this is extra important consideration to start early. Your guideline for starting the seeds and planting in the garden is the date of the final frost in spring. If your growing season is short, you should start the seeds eight weeks before this date. If you experience long summers, you can start six weeks prior to the final frost.

Tomato seeds will germinate much faster and be able to grow healthy roots if the soil in their seedling trays is warm enough. The soil temperature must be kept between seventy and ninety degrees Fahrenheit, and should not vary too much. If your seed trays have individual compartments, plant two seeds in each, but if the tray does not have compartments, plant them half an inch apart. As soon as they start sprouting, move them to a sunny area, preferably a sunny south facing window. Otherwise, provide the strong light they need by installing an artificial light source. Tomatoes certainly love warmth and will quickly react to a lack of warmth and light by growing weak and thin. This stress may also make them more susceptible to diseases.

Within the first week or so the first embriotic leaves, called cotyledon leaves will make an appearance. True leaves, however will not likely appear before one month or longer. When a set of these true leaves has emerged it is time to gently transplant the seedlings into their individual containers. You should bury them up to the line of their cotyledon leaves so that they can grow more roots, thus develop into strong seedlings. Keep the temperature at around seventy degrees F until they reach the stage when they are developed enough to be planted into your garden.

Delay the transplanting of your tomato seedlings into your garden if there is any danger of more frost. Measure the soil temperature; it must be at least fifty degrees F, but of course the warmer the soil, the better your plants will adjust to their new surroundings. If you do not have a thermometer, be aware that the temperature in the atmosphere around you do not always coincide with that of the soil, it may vary due to the wetness of the soil. Take care not to subject your plants to cold stress if you want to harvest juicy, healthy fruit later in the season.

4.   Tomato Plants Need Sunlight

All plants need sunlight for photosynthesis, the process in which they make nutrients in their leaves. Plants that bear fruit need as much sunlight as possible to manufacture enough food for growing their flavorful, juicy tomatoes; their demand for light is high. Exposure to six hours of light a day will result in a moderate fruit yield but even eight hours might not even be enough for those juicy tomatoes you anticipate, so inspect your garden for the area with the most sunlight during the growing season. A location with lots of light will give you the quantity and quality of fruit you want.

Tomato plants that lack enough light will develop spindly stems as they seek more sun. They will be prone to all kinds of diseases and pests. The greatest threads are the fungal diseases that flourish in cooler, wet conditions. It is a fact that the more sunlight the plant gets, the more flavorful the fruit it bears. Tomatoes love heat; they will even thrive in desert-like areas where they get full sun the whole daylong. If you live in such an area and you provide you plants with proper irrigation, you will be able to grow delicious, juicy tomatoes.

Do not despair if your area is not sunny enough; you can make use of artificial light. The lights must be bright and should be adjusted from time to time to make sure the entire plant is exposed to enough light as it grows.

5.   Tomato Plants Need Rich Soil

You have selected the location with the most sunlight for your plant. Now you have to consider the type of soil in area. Tomatoes need an abundance of nutrients at all times. You can supply this in the form of soluble fertilizer, but this means that they get heavy doses at certain intervals, rather than a steady supply of food. Therefore, the ideal situation to grow them is a well-cultivated bed with rich soil. Use quality compost in the soil to fortify it. I have seen tomato plants thriving in a compost heap, yielding better fruit than their well-tended counterparts in pots or beds in the garden.

If you choose a pot to grow your tomato plant in, go for the large one. Fill the pot with lots of organic material like manure, leaf mold and compost to encourage strong root growth. To supply your plant with a continuous supply of nutrients, use organic fertilizers such as blood meal, bone meal and fish emulsion that will release the nutrients slowly over a long period. Your pot also needs good aeration and drainage, so add gritty materials like vermiculite to the mixture.

Tomato plants need magnesium and calcium. You can either mix Epsom salt and bone meal into the soil of your pot, or add dolomite, which is a natural supplement of limestone minerals. If you decide to use the latter, test the pH level of your soil because dolomite can raise the alkaline level. Some people use coffee grounds but these might also lead to excessive alkalinity if you add too much. I always pack the top surface of the soil with crushed eggshells as they prevent pests with soft bodies from reaching the plant and slowly release the calcium into your plant's soil.

6.   Seedling Should Be Planted Deep

Do not be over-eager to transplant your tomato seedlings into their beds in the garden. Wait until they are about six inches high and have more than two true leaves. Move them outside from time to time to harden them over a period of seven day, gradually exposing the young plants to the sunlight and outside conditions until they are spending the whole day outside. As soon as the night temperature is high enough, plant them into pockets in the beds. Line the hole with any organic material, for instance bone meal or kelp meal mixed together with some compost.

Make the holes in the beds deep enough so that the entire roots systems and a part of their stems are covered. In the case of seedlings that have already grown too tall, you can remove some of the lowest branches or leaves using a well-sharpened blade and plant them deeper in the holes. The tomato plants need to be anchored well with strong root systems. Planting them deeper into the soil will allow them to develop more roots to give them that strong base they need.

Sometimes tomato plants are planted into the soil horizontally. This is usually done in areas with a colder climate and a much shorter growing season. All the lower leaves and branches are removed and the plants are then placed in a shallow trench. The entire plant except the top growth is covered with soil to help keep the plant warm and allow roots to grow from the entire main stem of the plant. Only the top cluster of leaves remain outside the soil. The result of this extended root system is a good harvest later on.

7.   Give the Plant Extra Warmth

Most tomato plants flourish in a warm climate. They love the heat and do well in temperatures ranging between sixty to eighty degrees F in the day and night temperatures higher than fifty degrees F. The more heat they receive, the better the quality of the fruit, especially if you want flavorful ones. In areas further north with lower temperatures, try to provide the root zones of your plants with extra heat as this will ensure a strong extended root system which in turn will yield fleshy, large tomatoes.

Place black plastic mulch into the soil of your beds before you plant the seedlings into them. The soil will warm up much faster when covered with the plastic. Make slits into the plastic to plant the seedlings. The warmer soil will help the roots to grow stronger and protect them from unexpected frost or freezes. Some gardeners use aluminum foil to cover the area around each plant to reflect even more warm sunlight on the plant and to cover the soil around it. Additionally, it prevents pests from coming near your seedlings. Red Plastic tomato mulch is thinner than the black mulch and could be used later on. It prevents weeds from growing, also retains the heat of the soil and help uniform ripening of your harvest.

8.   Lush Growth as Your Target

Some plants will grow regardless of poor soil and neglect but tomatoes thrive on tender loving care. If you give them enough attention, they will repay you with plump, luscious fruit.

Most importantly, you should provide them with aerated, rich soil so that they can develop a strong, abundant root system. This in turn will encourage the top part of the plant to grow healthy, sturdy branches and will reward your efforts with plenty of flavor-filled tomatoes. If your plant has fat, strong stems with the nodes closely placed, it shows that they are healthy and happy with their treatment. Spindly, thin branches indicate a lack of adequate sunlight and nutrients. Unhealthy plants will easily be prone to diseases and breakages. You should always stake them right from the start.

Generally, bigger plants will yield more fruit. However, an overabundance of nitrogen in the plant's soil will lead to plants with lots of vegetative growth but less flowers and fruit yield. Therefore, if your healthy, vigorous plant does not grow any flowers, you should pinch the tips. Adding phosphorous fertilizer will also help to solve the problem.

9.   Water Stress

While your tomato plants are in their growing phase, they need lots of water. However, do not water them daily. What they need is regular deep watering. How frequently you do this, will depend on the climate in your area: the humidity, wind, and temperature.

Remove some of the top soil to test the dampness of the lower layer. During the hottest hours of the summer day, your plant might appear slightly wilted. This is normal, but if it does not recover during the coolness of the afternoon and early evening, it is an indication of water stress. A stressed plant will more easily succumb to infections, fungal or otherwise.

Too much watering while the plant is bearing fruit might result in split tomatoes. A little water stress might even enhance the flavor of the fruit. A plentiful rainy season may dilute their flavor, so it is essential that your plants have adequate drainage.

10.   Trim Plants for Tastier, Larger Tomatoes

Determinate, or bushy plants, have limited growth and will, in most instances, not need any trimming to start flowering and bearing fruit. Once they reach their normal height, they will go about the process without any intervention from you. However, the indeterminate, or vining tomato kind, will need some trimming so that they can transfer their growth effort into bearing fruit instead of growing the branches and foliage. As soon as summer starts, pinch all the tips of the main branches.

Sometimes tomato plants develop many small branches off the main ones. These are not needed since they will yield inferior fruit and should be trimmed to allow for growth where it is really needed. All the nutrients and energy of your plant should be channeled towards its main parts, like the larger branches and fruit. Also, remove all lower leaves that are in the shade and may overtax the plant. Do this regularly.

11.   Sweet Soil Means Sweet Fruit

Tomato plants are quite happy in soil that is slightly acidic but as soon as your tomatoes start to ripen, increase the alkaline level of their soil to ensure sweeter fruit. Raise the pH levels by adding wood ash. Additionally, it is a good supplier of potassium. This mineral helps to produce more sugars in the plant as well as assist with its transportation to the fruit. Potassium also increases production of lycopene, which is the bright red pigment in tomatoes. Lycopene is a carotenoid and a potent antioxidant.

If you cannot lay your hands-on wood ash, consider using limestone/dolomite. It supplies magnesium and calcium to the plant soil. Experienced home gardeners have been known to apply baking soda, a quick fixer for the reduction of tartness in their tomatoes.

A Last Word

Ultimately, trial and error is the best way to find your favorite variety of tomato and decide which cultivars grow best in your area. We are all individuals with our own preferences. I am sure, however, that these tips will provide you with enough knowhow to get on with the business on hand and ensure that you will have the juiciest, most tasty tomatoes to enjoy in your dishes.

Chapter Four:

The Ripening and Harvesting of Tomatoes

You are one of the fortunate people who are in a position to grow their own juicy tomatoes. The next question to consider is when exactly to harvest them. Usually we just look at the color of the fruit and make our decision accordingly; a bright red color is the indication that the fruit should now be picked. However, this might not be the wisest decision to make. Color can be misleading; by the time the tomato is red all over it might be too late.

1.   When to Harvest Tomatoes

Tomatoes emit a natural gas called ethylene; they are gassy fruit. Mature, fully formed green tomatoes produce this gas. When two different growth hormones inside the tomato start producing gas, it results in the aging of the cells. Ethylene decreases the production of chlorophyll, which means losing its green color and increases the yellow and red color, or carotenoids, of the fruit. It also leads to the softening of the tomatoes.

This is the reason why tomatoes are amongst the few vegetables (although it is actually classified as a fruit) that can be harvested when it has not yet completely ripened. Ideally, tomatoes should be picked when they are mature but still green. They will then ripen off the plant. Picking the tomatoes while they are still green will prevent bruising and splitting, and give you some control over the duration of the process of ripening.

2.   How Should I Harvest My Tomatoes

The tomatoes we buy in supermarkets are usually picked even before they are fully mature to allow them to ripen while being transported. These tomatoes do not have the same flavor as those that are left on the vines a little longer. Pick your tomatoes when they are still green but fully matured for the best flavor. Generally, harvest time is towards the end of summer, at the end of the fruits' growing season.

How do you know when a tomato is fully mature? Check for the beginning of a light blush starting to show, before it actually starts to change color; this will be the indication that the fruit is ready to be picked. This subtle change in color will start at the bottom of the tomato, especially in the bigger heirloom varieties. Tomatoes left to ripen completely on the plant will still be the most flavorful, so of course you can wait until they are bright yellow or red.

Just keep your eye on them; some tomatoes may split or crack and some varieties will be too plump and heavy for the branches. If you are still in doubt when to pick a fully ripened tomato, put one in water; if it sinks to the bottom, it is ready. You can also squeeze the tomato lightly without bruising it, to test its firmness.

To harvest tomatoes is easy. Take the fruit in one hand firmly but be gentle, while holding on to the stalk with the other hand. Pull the tomato to break the stalk above the calyx.

If you have picked green tomatoes, you are now in control of the ripening process. If you want to hasten the process, you can do the following: Wrap them up in newspaper, which will keep the gas emitted by the fruit contained and so hasten the ripening process. A warmer temperature will also help to ripen them quicker. If you are not in a hurry and want to keep your tomatoes for a while, store the fruit at a temperature of less than 55 degrees F. The average temperature for storage is between 55 and 70 degrees F, or 13 to 21 degrees Celsius.

3.   How to Make Them Turn Red

If the temperature is too high, above 86 degrees F, tomatoes will not turn red. If the summers in your area are very hot, you should pick your fruit while they are still green or pink and then allow them to ripen under the cooler conditions indoors. If you leave them on the vine too long, the high temperatures will turn them yellowish orange.

Tomatoes do not need light to be able to ripen, only heat. Rather than putting them in the sun on your windowsill, store them in a cool area with temperatures of between 65 and 70m degrees F. You may even place them inside a dark vegetable cupboard.

4.   Harvesting During a Time of Frost

The weatherman has just predicted the first frost while you still have loads of green fruit on your tomato plant. We all know that tomatoes will not weather frost, but do not panic. The first frost is usually a light one, so you will be able to protect your plants from this onslaught. Cover all your plants with one of the follow overnight: plastic, old sheets, big boxes or burlap bags. It might be a little effort, but worth your trouble since the next frost often only occurs two or three weeks later and by that time, your tomatoes will be ready for harvesting.

If a sudden heavy freeze is predicted, you have only one choice; immediately go and harvest all your tomatoes. The small green tomatoes, although not ripe yet, can be cooked green or pickled. Those that have reached three quarter of their mature size and start to show a little color can successfully be ripened indoors. If you follow these guidelines, you will not lose any of your harvest.

I know of people who unearth the entire plant to hang upside down in their dark garage or basement. The tomatoes will gradually ripen but take care that they do not ripen and fall to the floor without your noticing it. Check on them regularly and pick any ripe ones in time.

5.   Ripening Tomatoes on a Shelf

An easy way to ripen green tomatoes is to place them, covered in newspaper sheets, on shelves. You may wrap them individually, but that will test your patience when you have to unwrap every one each day to check their color. It is important to check on them regularly not only to take out the ripe ones, but also to discard any fruit that have started to rot. Covering them in these sheets will trap the ethylene gas they emit and so hasten the ripening process. Other fruits like apples and bananas also produce this natural gas and placing your tomatoes in paper bags with one of them, is another method of speeding up the ripening process.

6.   Autumn Tomatoes

Fall tomatoes can successfully be grown in some parts of southwestern and southern states of the country. The only real problem you may encounter is to find young plants for sale during summer.

This need not deter you; the problem can be solved by cutting the small suckers off your spring plants. Allow them to grow to their full size. Do not pinch out all the offshoots from your plant; leave a few to grow up to five inches. When summer nears its end, cut a few shoots, discard the bottom set of foliage and put them in moistened vermiculite or sand, or in a jar with water. They will start rooting and as soon as a few roots are out, you can plant them straight into your garden or in pots. Press down the soil all around your plant firmly and give them plenty of water for the next couple of days.

These tomato plants will grow equally well as those you raise from seeds or purchase at your local nursery. Check well for any insects or diseases, otherwise you will be stuck with the problem for the entire fall. Now you can have a wonderful autumn crop of fruit in your own garden.

Chapter Five

The Preservation of Tomatoes

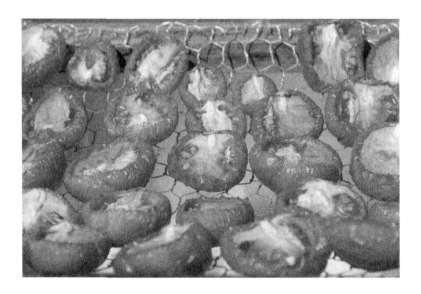

Drying Tomatoes

What a great satisfaction it is to enjoy the fruits of summer long after all traces of the season are gone. We seem to appreciate them even more as we progress into the colder winter months. The strong aroma and intense flavor of freshly picked tomato cannot be surpassed. However, what to do if the end of the season leaves you with more fruit than you and your friends can use. Your pleasure at the bounty of your crop can quickly turn into a feeling of despair if you are burdened with armfuls of tomatoes to deal with.

Fortunately, you are not the first person faced with this dilemma. People long before you had to come up with a solution purely out of necessity; nobody wants to see their hours of loving attention and hard work go to waste. Therefore, the art of preserving was born. Fresh tomatoes can easily and quickly be frozen but once defrosted they will have a texture which is quite mealy. Canning is not an easy process although storing cans is quite economical.

Both canning and freezing tomatoes call for extreme temperatures. On the other hand, to drying tomatoes is a much gentler approach. It is really simple to do and a very rewarding task. When tomatoes are dried, they lose most of their moisture, concentrating their flavor and bring to light their berrylike essence. Even tomatoes of a lesser flavor can be enhanced this way.

Long before the days of freezers and canning equipment, people had already started to dry tomatoes. It is definitely the oldest method of preservation. Since you only need the energy of the sun for a few days, it is easy and simple to follow this traditional method. The result will be sweet-tart, chewy fruit with intense flavor and unbelievable versatility.

Selection and Preparation

Although all the different varieties of tomatoes are suitable for drying, for your first attempt select those with thicker, meaty skins, less gel and fewer seeds, for instance the beefsteak or salad type. The best traditional kind for drying is the Principe Borghese. If you intend to make paste with your dried tomatoes, use La Roma and for sauces, use San Marzano, the Italians' favorite. To add color to your plate, try Lemon Boy, a bright yellow tomato, or Italian Gold, for a vibrant orange. I would also like to suggest two cherry tomato varieties; Sweet 100 and Sungold. They are rich in acids and sugars that provide the dried product with a candy-like, piquant taste.

When you make your selection, be sure to choose those fruit that are ripe, but still firm. They must be without any blemish or damage and not overripe, lest they become spoiled and infect other fruit as well. Do not blanch them; they only need washing and drying. You want your fruit to dry evenly, so cut them uniformly. Plum-like fruit can be halved or quartered lengthwise while cherry tomatoes can be cut into halves or left whole. Larger types can be sliced a half or quarter inch thick. To yield one ounce of the dried product, you have to dry around a pound of the fresh fruit.

Sun-Drying, the Traditional Way

The weather will have to play its part if you want to try this method. What you need is consecutive dry and sunny days, not warmer than around 95 degrees, as well as low humidity, (lower than twenty percent). The area you choose should have full sun right through the day. If you have a flagstone patio or a paved area which will reflect the rays of the sun, so much the better.

Buy a mesh screen from a cookware shop. It has to be plastic because metal wire will react to the tomato acids and may spoil the flavor. Spread your tomatoes out on the screen in one layer, placing them about one inch apart to allow air to circulate around each fruit. To protect your tomatoes from birds and insects, cover with cheesecloth. Your trays should be lifted a foot or more from the ground to help the air circulation. Do not leave your trays outside when rain is forecast. Tomatoes will take between three to seven days to dry to their soft, leathery consistency, all depending on factors like the weather, their moister content and thickness.

Oven-Drying, the Easy Way

If the weather does not play along, you can always fall back on the convenient method of oven drying. Either an electric or gas oven will work perfectly. Your oven should be on its lowest setting. In case your oven does not go below the 150 degrees setting, do not worry; you can slow roast the tomatoes with equally satisfying results. Again, depending on the moister content and size of your fruit, it will take around six to twelve hours in the oven. The temperature of your oven will also influence the time it will take to dry. If your dried tomatoes still contain too much moisture, you will not be able to store them for too long, but drier products with less moisture can successfully be stored for a much longer period. You want a leathery, pliant product for the best overall results.

Preheat your oven to around 140 degrees F. Gently squeeze some of the seeds from the tomato halves and place them cut-side up on a parchment lined cookie sheet. Leave your oven door slightly open so that the hot moist air can escape. After a couple of hours, check on your tomatoes. You can turn them over and press down on them lightly with a spatula. Repeat this process until they are leathery and the edges have curled slightly. They should not be sticky after they have cooled down.

If you prefer a juicier fruit with a richer flavor, you can remove the tomatoes earlier. In that case, the fruit will have to be refrigerated. Put them in a jar with olive oil. In the refrigerator, they will keep for as long as six weeks.

Effortless Dehydrating

To obtain the ultimate, uniform results, you will have to make use of an electric dehydrator. Convection ovens with a very low setting are equally effective. The heating elements of dehydrators give you the low temperatures of 140 degrees F you desire, as well as the low humidity to ensure proper drying. If you decide to purchase a dehydrator, invest in one with temperature controls, a timer and a fan. With this method, the drying process will take between five to nine hours resulting in fruits which are dried evenly and which can be stored for long periods.

As mentioned above, a convection oven is another option, as long as it has a temperature setting of between 110 and 140 degrees F. Its capacity will be less, however. Always follow the instructions from the manufacturer. Microwave ovens are not suitable for drying tomatoes as they neither provide air circulation, nor a continuous moderate heat which are both essential.

Uses and Storage

Dried tomatoes should be cooled down to room temperature before they can be stored. Store them in airtight bags to maintain the moisture content of the fruit; although it is already low, you do not want them to dry out entirely. Get rid of all excess air in the bag. Now they can be stored for as long as eight months if you keep them in a cool, (sixty to seventy degrees F) dark area. In the refrigerator, they will keep for the same length of time. Frozen dried tomatoes will keep for a year.

Dried tomatoes have a myriad of uses; they make a delicious addition to salads and add a wonderful flavor to pasta or sauces. Chop them up and add to your sandwich filling or cut into julienne slivers to mix with a Mediterranean vegetable dish. They can also quickly and easily be rehydrated. Just cover them completely with either warm water or even wine and leave them to soak for around ten minutes. They will be plump and soft and enhance any dish.

Slow Roasted Tomatoes

Oven drying means that you literally dry out your tomatoes until most of the moisture is gone. Slow roasting on the other hand is a gentle cooking process that leaves the juices caramelized. This technique is ideal if you are pressed for time or do want to purchase an electrical dehydrator. The only disadvantage is a shorter storage time. Do not keep them longer than a week inside your refrigerator or 6 months in your freezer.

This method is easy and simple. Set your oven for 225 degrees F. Spread out your tomatoes on a parchment lined cookie sheet with their skin sides down. I like to dress my tomatoes with herbs like thyme, rosemary, marjoram or oregano for extra flavor. Season them with salt and pepper. If you prefer a more spicy-sweet taste, drizzle some flavored oil like orange or lemon on the tomatoes, followed by cayenne pepper and granulated sugar.

Slow roasting will save you a lot of time; it takes only between two to four hours. Other than dried tomatoes, this method will leave you with moist and soft fruit. First, allow your tomatoes to cool down to room temperature, then store in airtight containers in the refrigerator. They are delicious and can be used in mashed potatoes, soups and pastas.

Freezing Tomatoes

Whether you choose this method of preserving your excess tomato crops will depend entirely on your freezer size and how much free space you have in it. You may need to keep the frozen product in it for some time, so keep in mind how much space you will need for other foodstuffs in the coming months.

Why Choose Freezing

It is always handy to have a few frozen portions of sauce in your freezer. You can add it to pasta dishes or other sauces to stretch them and provide extra flavor, and it is an easy, convenient way to preserve that excess sauce from your canning batch. Store it in separate containers, leaving about half an inch of space on the top of your containers.

You can actually start this during the summer. Wash the ripe tomatoes, and then cover them in boiling water for a few minutes or until the skin starts to split. This makes it easier to remove the skins. Now seed them before you go on to stew them. Remove from the heat, spread out onto a large tray to allow them to cool down to room temperature.

Sprinkle with a little bit of sugar. As soon as they have cooled down sufficiently, store them in containers in your freezer. When the winter arrives and your fresh tomatoes are mostly finished, you can simply take the frozen ones from your freezer to use in stews and sauces. You will thank yourself later since you have just saved a lot of hassle and time.

How Do I Freeze Tomatoes

If you are stuck with a large surplus of fruit, freeze them whole after scalding them for thirty seconds. The boiling water will loosen the skins of the tomatoes. The best fruit for freezing whole are the meaty ones. Remember that tomatoes are quite mushy after defrosting. Keep tomatoes unsliced or slice them, then arrange on cookie trays and put the trays on a level surface in your freezer. As soon as they are frozen solid, you can put them into containers back in the freezer.

Canning Tomatoes

Maybe you do not have enough space in your freezer for your excess crops. Canning is the answer. It does not take up a lot of space and is a trusted and easy method for saving the flavor of any variety of fresh tomato. Now I will tell you exactly how to go about it.

Using a Boiling Water Bath

Although canning is easy, you should always use the proper techniques for safety's sake. Vegetables with a low acid content require a pressure canner, but fortunately most tomato varieties are high in acid and can safely be canned using a water bath. However, this is not valid if you want to can tomato sauce that includes meat or vegetables; then the pressure canner is necessary to ensure the safety of the canned product.

If you decide to use a canner, follow all the instructions carefully: they may vary from canner to canner.

Assemble the Utensils

These are the utensils you will need: a canner with its rack, tongs or a jar lifter, mason jars, cooling racks, a timer, slotted spoon, non-metallic spatula and a wide-mouthed funnel.

Stick to mason jars when you can tomatoes. They are tried and tested and can be safely used because they are heat-tempered. They also seal perfectly and are easily available.

Dome lids should not be used for canning. The rubber seals will lose their capacity to seal properly after only one use whereas mason jars and metal screw bands can be used repeatedly.

Check and Clean the Equipment

Examine all jars to be used for cracks or chips. If using metal bands, check for dents, nicks or rust. Do not use them if they are not in pristine condition; damaged bands should rather be recycled.

You have to wash everything thoroughly, afterwards scalding the equipment in very hot water to remove all germs. Keep the screw tops and jars hot up to the time that you are using them. Prepare all metal lids by following the instructions of the manufacturer.

Select the Cleanest, Freshest Tomatoes

A bunch of tomatoes produces around eighteen quarts and 3 pounds of fruit will yield a quart. The yield will vary if you cook the tomatoes down for paste, juice or sauces.

All tomatoes should be washed thoroughly. To facilitate pealing, dunk them in boiling water for thirty seconds and then place them in a container with cold water. Carefully peel off their skins. Make sure not to use any unhealthy or overripe fruit and remove all the stems. Cut away any spots. You need only a single bad tomato to spoil the entire batch, similar to the bad apple.

Hot Pack in Water

You have cleaned your tomatoes and removed their skins. If they are quite large, cut them in two. Now place the halved or whole tomatoes in a saucepan with enough water to cover them completely. Allow them to boil for around five minutes. If using quart jars, put two tablespoons of lemon juice or a half-teaspoon of citric acid into each jar. For pint jars, use one tablespoon of lemon juice or a quarter teaspoon of the acid. You may add a pinch of salt if desired. Fill the hot jars one by one with the hot tomatoes, leaving some space on top. Pour the hot cooking liquid into each jar, still leaving a half-inch headspace. Wipe the rims of the jars clean, attach the lids and close.

Hot Pack Crushed Tomatoes

Cut about half of your tomatoes into quarters. Heat them in a pot, crushing them to release the juice. Stir until they come to the boil, and then add the remainder of the fruit a little at a time. There is no need to cut them up as well; they will soften in the process of cooking and stirring. Allow to cook gently for five minutes. Continue as described above, adding the lemon juice and citric acid before closing the lids and storing the containers.

Raw Pack

You will need liquid for your raw tomatoes when canning them, so prepare a homemade juice in advance. If you do not have time to prepare your own, simply use canned juice. For every pint, you will need a half to a three-quarter cup of liquid. In case you run short, refrain from adding water to your home-made juice; it will only lower the level of acidity in the tomato juice. Rather add canned juice.

After you have peeled the fruit, place them into the clean jars, pressing down gently to fit as many as possible into each jar. Make sure not to break them. They should fit snugly. Again, leave some space at the top. Add the same amount of lemon juice or citric acid as prescribed above to each jar. Make sure your juice is boiling hot before pouring it into each jar, filling it to about half an inch from the top. Use a knife to get rid of all the air bubbles in the jars, the less air in them the better. Wipe the rims of the mason jars and cover with the lids.

How to Store Canned Tomatoes

Store your canned tomatoes in a clean, dark place. The temperature should be cool, between fifty and seventy degrees F. Make sure the humidity in the storage area is low. Before your pack them away, label each jar with the date. It is easy to forget exactly when you canned your fruit later on, especially if you do it in two or more batches. Always move the oldest batch to the front of the shelf so that those jars would be used first. Try to consume your tomatoes within a year but if you overestimated your tomato crop and canned more than you bargained for, discard any leftovers before two years have passed.

Conclusion

Not only are tomatoes delicious and versatile, they are also extreme beneficial to your health. Because they contain high levels of lycopene, a natural antioxidant, they help slow down the growth of cancerous cells. The calcium and Vitamin K help to maintain strong bones and Vitamin A assists your immune system and help to maintain normal vision. Tomatoes are rich in Vitamin C, which is important for wound healing. Their Vitamin B and potassium content will help your body to reduce cholesterol and lower your blood pressure.

Tomatoes can be used in so many different ways. They are probably best eaten fresh in salads or on sandwiches, but are equally delicious in an omelet or frittata. Who can imagine a pizza without tomato? Or a rich chili sauce? Use them in summer or winter soups or in your homemade salsa and dips like guacamole.

Your friends will love you for your gifts of fresh tomatoes and envy your beautiful tomato plants. Tomatoes preserved in olive oil, garlic and a variety of herbs like oregano, basil and thyme will make a wonderful hostess gift. You can entertain your family and friends with your homegrown tomatoes with their interesting, exotic names like Adoration, Big Rainbow, Flamenco, Green Zebra, Hillbilly and Traveler.

Many people all over the world have learned the benefits of growing their own tomato plants. Now it is your turn.

Other Related Books

ISBN-13: 978-1601383501

ISBN-13: 978-1517773762

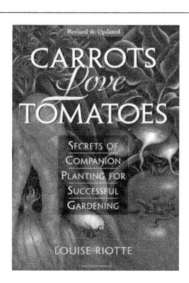

ISBN-13: 978-1580170277

ISBN-13: 978-1517646363

ISBN-13: 978-1533178862

ISBN-13: 978-1463727116